SPECIALS!

STUDY SKILLS

Jeanne Holloway

Folens Publishers

Acknowledgements

Post-it® Notes is a registered trademark of 3M.

© 1995 Folens Limited, on behalf of the author.

First published 1995 by Folens Limited, Albert House, Apex Business Centre, Boscombe Road, Dunstable, Beds, LU5 4RL, England.

ISBN 1 8527 6859

Editor: Catherine Miller.   Layout Artist: Suzanne Ward.

Illustrations: Eric Jones.   Cover photo: Image Bank.

Printed by Ashford Colour Press.

Contents

Introduction

The activities in this book have been formulated to enable pupils to practise and improve skills that are vital to all areas of study: the process skills of learning. Pupils do not acquire these skills fortuitously; they need, firstly, to be taught them, and secondly, to be given the opportunity to practise them.

The 'step-by-step' approach of these activity sheets allow pupils to gain confidence in these 'process of learning' skills. Each one allows the pupil to transfer the skill being practised to a real learning situation. Pupils and teachers are also encouraged to identify the kind of help and further practice each pupil needs.

A collaborative learning approach is further encouraged by the use of a partner or 'Study Buddy'. This helps ensure that pupils accomplish skills transfer in a non-threatening atmosphere.

The activity sheets are concerned with the primary skills of basic study:

1. Finding your way around a book (pages 6–19)
These activities engage pupils in active reading. They learn to skim and scan and search for information.

2. Note-making and paragraphs (pages 20–22)
These activities involve pupils in brainstorming and collecting sets of thoughts that go together. They also learn to reject material they do not want. The pupils learn how to utilise various forms of diagrams in note-making and paragraph formulation. They learn how to select key words and relate reading purpose to outcome. They also learn how to use a key word approach to their own form of shorthand.

3. Memory training (pages 23–25)
This section involves pupils in making a diagram or a title/label for chapters of a book. This can be done on Post-it Notes. Then, using the Post-its as nudge cards, they recall the text extracts read, giving as much detail as possible. This also applies to the use of diagrams and illustrations. Simplifying a text involves pupils in selecting key words and using these as memory triggers. A spelling page includes a list of commonly mis-spelled words, together with strategies for remembering them.

4. Awareness of language (pages 26–29)
These activity sheets enable pupils to discover ways of extending simple language, select relevant language and give alternative choices. They also look at different sorts of language.

5. Structure and style (pages 30–35)
These give pupils an understanding of what is meant by the terms 'structure' and 'style' as they look at both poetry and prose.

6. Fact or opinion (pages 36–39)
This section includes activities that encourage the pupils to think about points of view, omission and detecting bias.

7. Revision techniques (pages 40–48)
Search-reading, formulating questions and reading to find answers all result in 'nudge packs' of questions and answers that can be tried out with a Study Buddy. Mnemonics are offered as a way of memorising information. Testing techniques are also offered.

As they acquire the skills of identifying their study goals, pupils should learn to formulate their own strategies for reading and selecting information. The activities in this book encourage active participation in the process of learning, emphasising the importance of discussion and self-evaluation, showing that learning can be fun.

A Study Skills Kit

● Check that you have everything necessary to study properly.

● Write down how you think the Study Skills Kit can help you.

Post-it Notes	For marking important parts of a text.
Felt-tipped pens	
Highlighter pens	For picking out key words.
Small cards	
Study Buddy	

The contents page

Can you tell what a book is about without reading it?

- Look at the covers and the contents pages of the two books below.
- Discuss with your Study Buddy what kind of books they are and what they could be about. Write down your thoughts.

THE SPIDER

Chapter 1 The Room
Chapter 2 No Entry
Chapter 3 Desperate Remedies
Chapter 4 Snow at last
Chapter 5 Closed Doors

GREEK AND ROMAN LIFE

Any clues in the title?

1 The Home
2 The Family
3 Dress
4 Education
5 Marriage

- Choose another book. Read the title. Read the contents page.
  Do not look on the back cover.
  Tell your Study Buddy what the book is about.
  How can you find out if you are right?

SPECIALS! Study Skills

Exploring one page

● Read this extract:

... he left the room. She followed. The guests looked on, dismayed, as they disappeared.

● Draw the 'story' from the extract, before discussing it with your Study Buddy.

● What did your Study Buddy draw?
● Did the word 'disappear' mean the same for both of you? Talk and write about it.

For me, 'disappear' meant _____

For my Study Buddy, 'disappear' meant _____

● What does this suggest about the way people read?

● Each choose a page from a story book. Draw it so that it tells your Study Buddy what that page is about.

Exploring one more page

This is how you search-read. Follow the steps below.

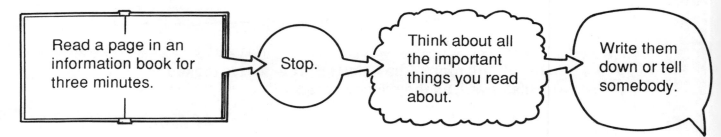

Read a page in an information book for three minutes. → Stop. → Think about all the important things you read about. → Write them down or tell somebody.

MY STUDY BUDDY IS

- Try it with this picture first. Be ready to tell your Study Buddy as many things as you can after three minutes.

Search for information

Pick out important things only.

Look for important details.

NOW

- Choose a page from an information book and follow the steps.
- Which one of you was better at search-reading?

NOTES _____

_____

_____

_____

_____

SPECIALS! Study Skills

Exploring a chapter

If you read the beginning and the end of a chapter, can you tell
what happens in the middle?

> **BEGINNING** ➤ He stared at the monster. It glared back at him, its huge
> eyes reflecting the light. Steam issued slowly from the
> cracks in between its ....

● Ask yourself some questions and give reasons for your answers.
  Is the monster:

A DRAGON ?	A BIG BUILDING?	A PERSON ?

> **ENDING** ➤ Finally, he slept.

● Why did he sleep? _____

● Have your views changed about the monster? Why? _____

● Write or draw what you think happened in the middle:

_____
_____
_____
_____
_____

● Choose a book. Let your Study Buddy choose a chapter.
  Read the beginning and end in this way and guess the middle.
  Then read and check. Were you right?

Writing blurb

'Blurb' is found on the back cover of a book. It tries to persuade us to read a book. It makes us want to know more.

- With a Study Buddy, choose two short stories for younger children that you can read fairly quickly.
- Write a blurb for each. Never give away the whole story!

MY BLURB...

MY STUDY BUDDY'S BLURB...

- Compare your blurbs.
- What does your Study Buddy say that would tempt a younger child to want to read the book?
- What do you say?

_____

_____

_____

- Read the blurbs of four short story books. List reasons why you would or would not want to read the whole books.
- Write some blurbs for books you have already read. Are your blurbs better than the originals?

The way around a dictionary

- Put a Post-it at the edge of pages that mark the end of each letter section of a dictionary.
- Talk with your Study Buddy about what you notice.

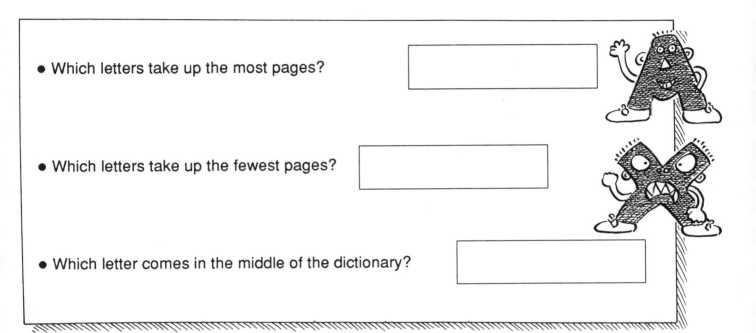

- Which letters take up the most pages?

- Which letters take up the fewest pages?

- Which letter comes in the middle of the dictionary?

}A to D

}E to M

}N to R

}S to Z

REMEMBER..
M
IS IN
THE
MIDDLE

- With your Study Buddy, collect ten guide words from the top of dictionary pages. Write them on small cards from your Study Skills Kit.
- How quickly can each of you collect the ten words?
  (Prove you really did by writing the page number next to each word!)

Dictionary blues

- Look up the word 'blue' in a dictionary.
- List all the blue words you can find:

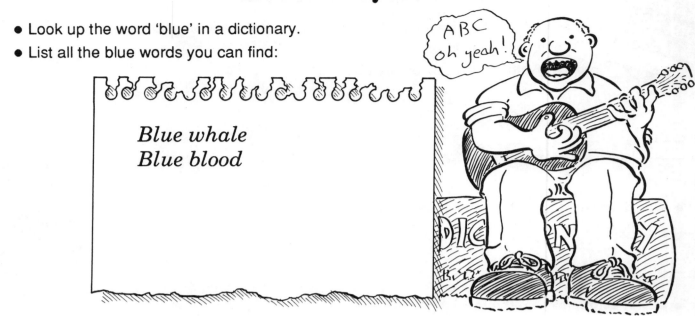

Blue whale
Blue blood

- Choose another colour word to look up.
  List your words here:

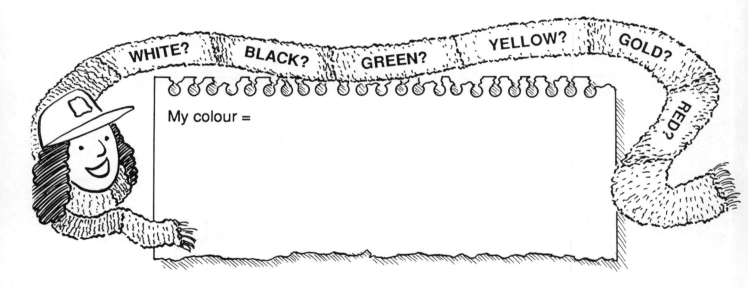

WHITE? BLACK? GREEN? YELLOW? GOLD? RED?

My colour =

- Compare your list with other people. Whose box has the most words?
- Look up some more colour words.
  Why do you think the name of a colour is attached to many words?

- With your Study Buddy, write about a character, using as many colour description words as you can.
- Make good use of your dictionary!

SPECIALS! Study Skills   © Folens

Brainstorming

- Choose a topic with your Study Buddy.
- Write down all the things that come to mind related to your topic – this is called brainstorming.

Topic:

- Brainstorm words to do with your topic:

YOU	YOUR STUDY BUDDY

- What did your Study Buddy write?
- Use different coloured pens to highlight sets of words that go well together.
- Cross out any words you do not want now.

- Using your 'colour coded' brainstorm, tell your Study Buddy about your topic or make up a story to write.
- Ask your Study Buddy to tell it in a different order. Does it work?

Brainstorming chart

- Choose a topic.
- Write the title of your topic in the biggest box below.
- Write the main points of your topic in the next biggest boxes.
- Write the less important points in the smallest boxes.

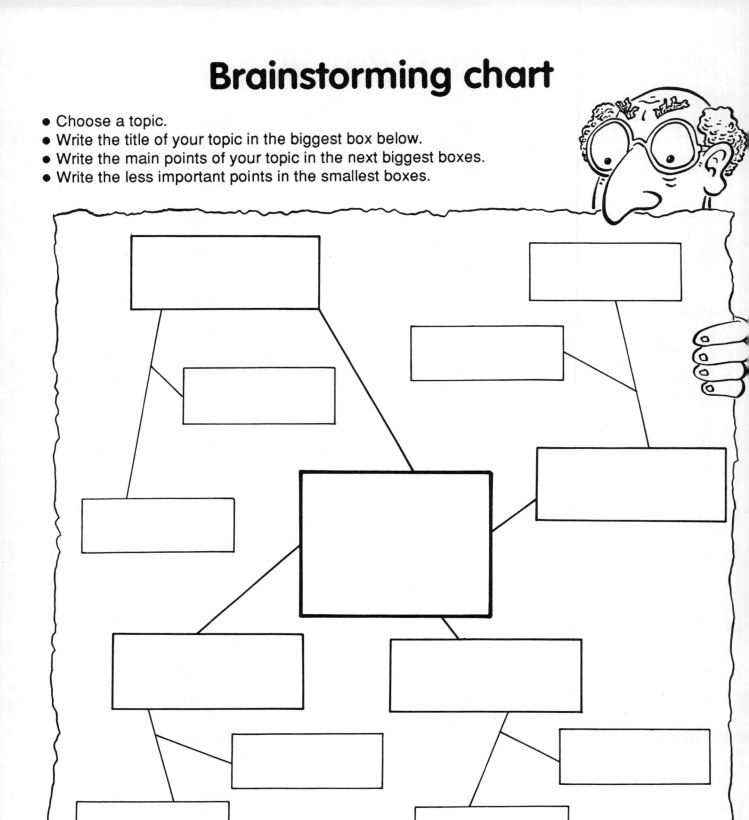

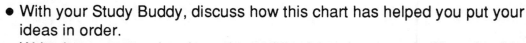

- With your Study Buddy, discuss how this chart has helped you put your ideas in order.
- Write four paragraphs about the main points of your topic. You should include the words in the smallest boxes.

SPECIALS! Study Skills   © Folens

Maps

What did you do on your way home from school yesterday?

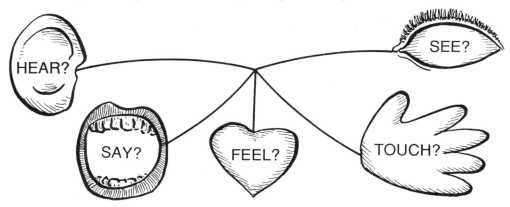

● Map it by drawing or writing below.

● Ask yourself: what could have affected the journey?

● Turn over and draw your own sequence of boxes like the ones in the diagram.
● Would your Study Buddy have made the same decisions?
Talk about this as you read your maps.

Mapping ideas

- Pick a topic and write it in the middle of a piece of paper.
- Write some information on the topic by answering these questions:

Who? What? Where? When? How? Why? Which?

- Try this one:

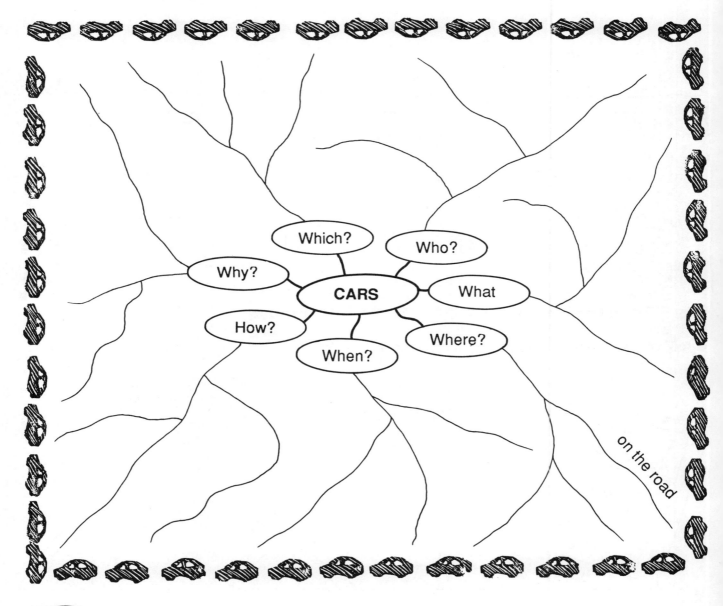

Which? Who?
Why? CARS What
How? Where?
When?

on the road

MY STUDY BUDDY IS

- With your Study Buddy, decide in what order you would write your notes in a paragraph.

SPECIALS! Study Skills © Folens

Shorthand

Secretaries often use 'shorthand'. Why?

- Can you understand the message above? If not, why not?
- What do you think the shorthand below says?

- With your Study Buddy, make up some more messages.

- Decide if they are useful.

- Let your Study Buddy choose a page from an information book.
- Make shorthand notes that you will still understand next week.

Key words

Key words are important for making summaries.
They are also important for revision.

Look at the words below for ten seconds.
Let your Study Buddy test your memory.

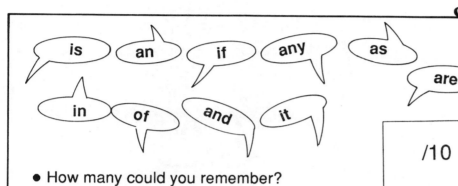

is   an   if   any   as

are

in   of   and   it

/10

● How many could you remember?

● Do the same for these words:

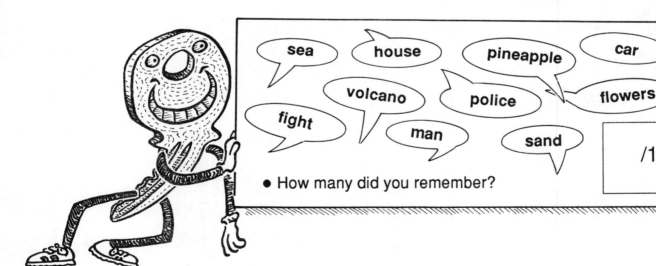

sea   house   pineapple   car

volcano   police   flowers

fight   man   sand

/10

● How many did you remember?

● Which set of words are you most likely to remember for:
  – a week
  – a month
  – a year?
● Why?

● With your Study Buddy, use the words in the second box to write
a story that could help you to remember them.

 SPECIALS! Study Skills

More key words

- Look at how to wire a plug in the British Isles.

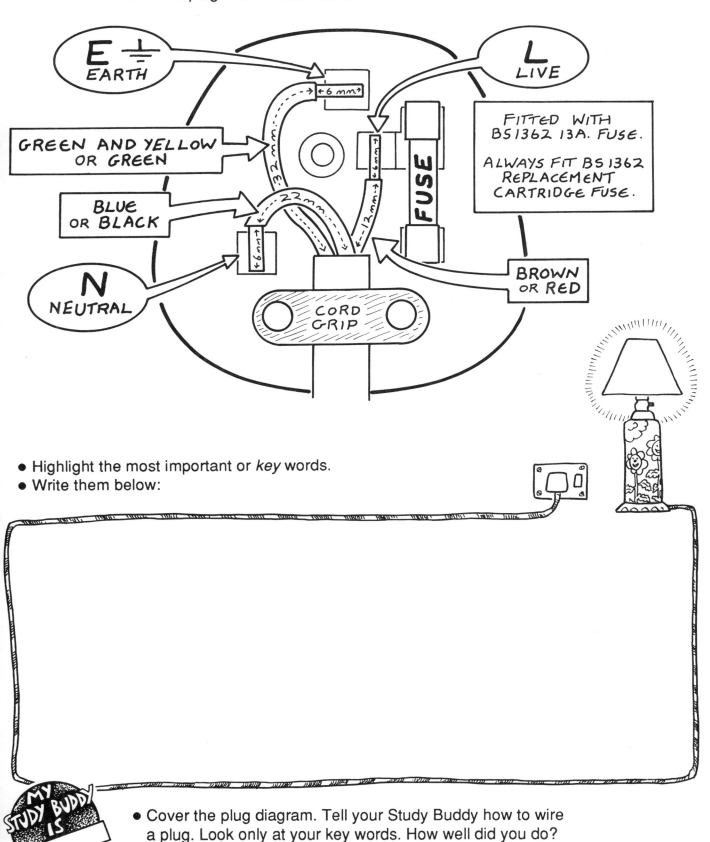

E ⏚
EARTH

GREEN AND YELLOW OR GREEN

BLUE OR BLACK

N
NEUTRAL

CORD GRIP

FUSE

L
LIVE

FITTED WITH BS1362 13A. FUSE.

ALWAYS FIT BS 1362 REPLACEMENT CARTRIDGE FUSE.

BROWN OR RED

← 6 mm →
← 6 mm →
32 mm
22 mm
12 mm
← 6 mm →

- Highlight the most important or *key* words.
- Write them below:

MY STUDY BUDDY IS

- Cover the plug diagram. Tell your Study Buddy how to wire a plug. Look only at your key words. How well did you do?

Drafting

This draft writing needs some spellings corrected and it is too short.

- Correct it and extend it by ten words.
  It has been started for you.

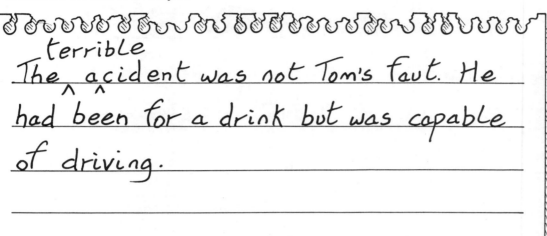

The terrible acident was not Tom's faut. He
had been for a drink but was capable
of driving.

- Write more about Tom. Who was he? What did he do?

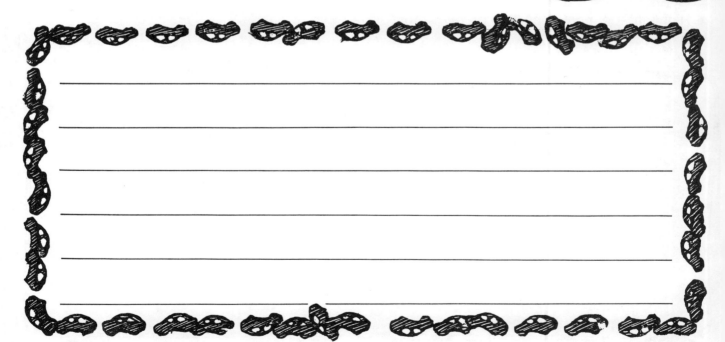

- Ask your Study Buddy to correct and extend your paragraph
  by a further ten words or more.

SPECIALS! Study Skills   © Folens

Paragraphs

A paragraph is a group of sentences about one topic or idea.

● Look at the brainstorm of words connected with animals.

trainer

pets

cruel

wild

circus — ANIMALS — experiments

police dogs

farm

zoo

vegetarians

● Add some of your own words to the brainstorm.

● Choose one of the words and write it down here:

● Turn over and collect other words to go with your choice.

● Connect the words to make three sentences. You have written a paragraph!

● Choose another word from the brainstorm. Write paragraphs with your Study Buddy using this method.
● Are they the same? If not, how are they different?

Understanding paragraphs

To write three paragraphs about

- In shape A, write three sentences about planets.
- In shape B, write three sentences about

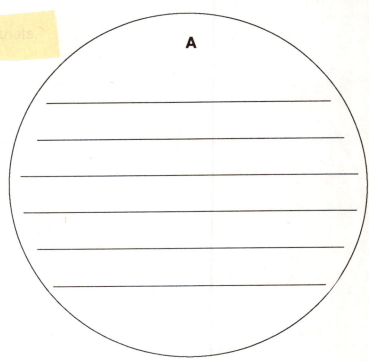

- In shape C, write three sentences about

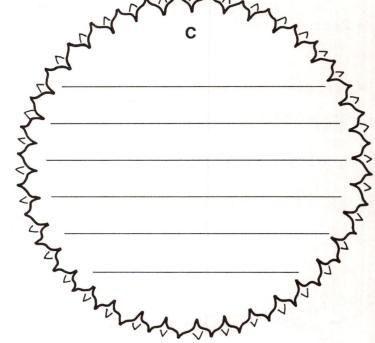

- Read your paragraphs to your Study Buddy in the order that sounds best.
- Draw three paragraph shapes for the title 'How to book a holiday' and write the paragraphs.

SPECIALS! Study Skills

Read, cover and remember a diagram

How can you remember diagram details?
Here are three steps to help you.

STEP ONE

- Look carefully at this diagram for ten seconds.

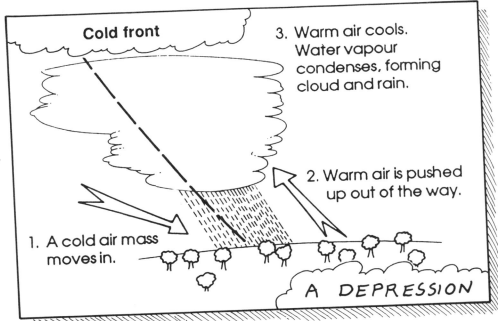

Cold front

3. Warm air cools. Water vapour condenses, forming cloud and rain.

2. Warm air is pushed up out of the way.

1. A cold air mass moves in.

A DEPRESSION

STEP TWO

- Cover it with a Post-it and write the key words on it.

STEP THREE

- Draw and write it out correctly while you say the key words.

MY STUDY BUDDY IS

- Repeat the three steps until your diagram is correct.
- Ask your Study Buddy to check your work.

NOW

- With your Study Buddy, find two labelled diagrams.
- Using the three steps, copy and label them.
- Correct in red any parts you keep getting wrong.
- Who remembers most?

Read, cover and remember text

- Choose one chapter of a book and make a title or 'label' for each page. Use Post-its.
- Practise first with this activity.

STEP ONE

Read it.

STEP TWO

Cover the part you want to remember with a Post-it and write the key words on it.

STEP THREE

Make a title or label for it below.

The ship was found in the Solent,

off Southsea Castle.

It had been there, preserved in

the silt, since 1545.

The *Mary Rose* had been

ready for battle.

TITLE

- Now, use the three steps for each page of the chapter you have chosen. You could make the label on the Post-it.

- With your Study Buddy, choose one more chapter. Use the three steps and label each paragraph of the *first* and *last* page of the chapter only.
- Tell your Study Buddy all you can from your Post-it notes.

SPECIALS! *Study Skills* © Folens

Some ways to remember spellings

- Look carefully at these words:

Fe<u>br</u>uary   **<u>acci</u>d<u>en</u>t**   **ne<u>ce</u>ss<u>ary</u>**

- You can spell them correctly by using 'memory trigger' words or drawings.

February

br it's cold

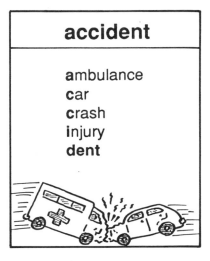

accident

ambulance
car
crash
injury
dent

necessary

one **c**ollar
two **s**hoes

- With your Study Buddy, make memory triggers for these words, or for difficult parts of the words.

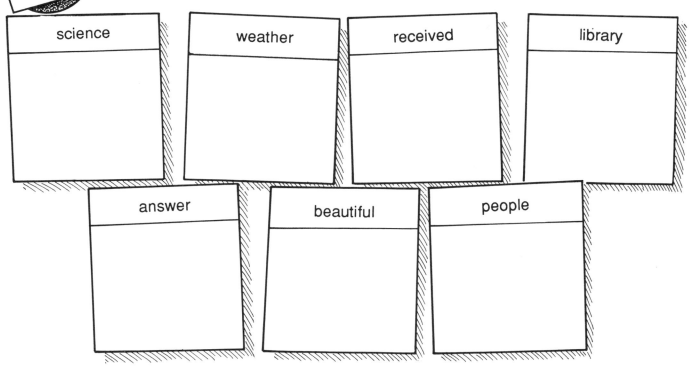

science

weather

received

library

answer

beautiful

people

- Ask your Study Buddy to test your spelling of these words.
- Highlight the parts of the words you are getting wrong. Do you need to make a new or better memory trigger? You could use colour and drawings.

Collecting connectives

Read these words. They are used to join ideas in sentences. They are called connectives.

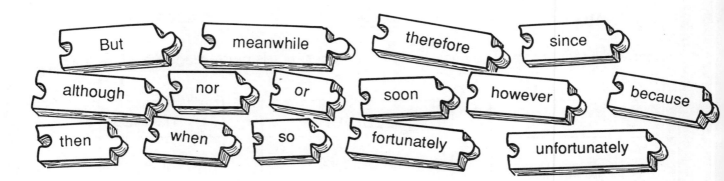

But   meanwhile   therefore   since
although   nor   or   soon   however   because
then   when   so   fortunately   unfortunately

● Write *two* sentences using *three* of them in the space below.

● With your Study Buddy, look in books to find more.
● Read this passage. How many times can you replace 'and' with another connecting word from this page (or with a full stop)?

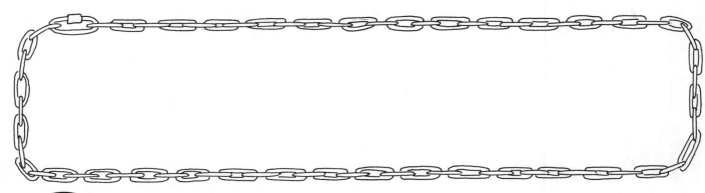

Dean stood at the bus stop and the bus came and he did not have his

money and he saw his friend on the bus and he got on and he did not

know if his friend could pay his fare and his mother had noticed his

money on the table and ran to the bus stop.

● With your Study Buddy, make up a story starting 'The storm began'. Use as many different connectives as you can.

A Study Buddy thesaurus

● Read this passage:

 She was a robber, bandit, brigand, highwayman, pickpocket, crook, shoplifter, swindler, burglar, housebreaker, pillager – in fact, she was a THIEF!

● How many different words were used to describe our thief?

● With your Study Buddy, brainstorm (write down all the different words that come to mind) alternative names for the following:

Teacher

Friend

Prison

● Write three short sentences about a teacher, a friend and a prison.
● Ask your Study Buddy to re-write them using some of the new words you have found.
● How are the meanings different?

Cloze activities

The [   ] began at midnight

like a bad dream. Jon only had one blanket, so he

was [   ] . He had curled up

like a [   ] to try and

keep warm, when he realised that [   ]

was pulling at his blanket. A terrible [   ]

filled his nostrils. It was the [   ] .

• Talk about your word choices.
• Which ones make the story most frightening?
• Can you think of words that could make the story funny?

• Write a six-sentence story describing a haunted house. Think about:
  – what the house looks like
  – what happens there.
• Ask your Study Buddy to re-write it, using other words for your descriptions but without changing the meaning.

Homophones

Read these words aloud:

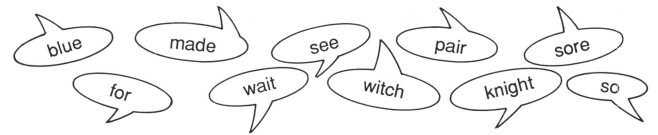

blue   made   see   pair   sore

for   wait   witch   knight   so

- Ask your Study Buddy to write them down as you read them out.
- How many different versions were there?

You might find these:
blew, weight, pear, four, which, sea, maid, night, saw, sew.

- Find ten more words that sound the same but can be spelled in more than one way. These words are called homophones.

Word	Homophone

Word	Homophone

- Select ten pairs of homophones and find ways of remembering which one is which. For example, 'blew' with a 'w' for *wind*. 'Witch with a 't' for *terrible*.

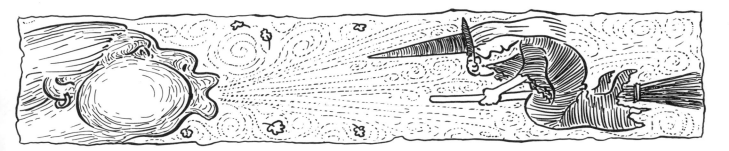

- Test each other on ten pairs of words.

Language – old and new

● Read these two examples of old English to your Study Buddy.

Al ful of joy and blisse is the paleys
and ful of instrumentz
and of vitaille
The most deyntevous of al Itaille.

Is this a dagger which I see before me
The handle toward my hand?
Come, let me clutch thee
I have thee not, and yet I see thee still.

● Underline in red the words you recognise.
● Underline in green any words that are spelled differently today.
● Underline in blue any unfamiliar words.
● What stops you understanding the examples?
● Choose one of the examples and translate it into modern English below. Compare your translation to your Study Buddy's.

● With your Study Buddy, talk about what influences English today.
● Think about the changing meanings of words. Think about what a word such as 'wicked' means to different people.

SPECIALS! Study Skills © Folens

Place names

- Read these place names:

Twickenham
Oldham
Newham

Rushton
Southampton
Luton

Ingoldsby
Laceby
Maltby

MY STUDY BUDDY IS

- With your Study Buddy, discuss why you think so many place names have similar endings.
- Use an atlas. Complete the chart with more place names.

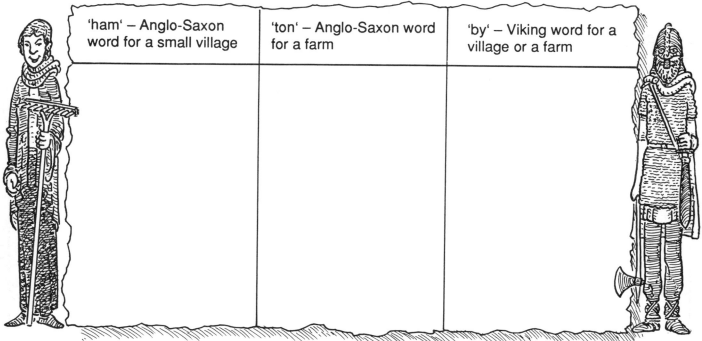

'ham' – Anglo-Saxon word for a small village	'ton' – Anglo-Saxon word for a farm	'by' – Viking word for a village or a farm

NoW

- With your Study Buddy update local place names to reflect the places as they are today.
- Where do names in your local area come from?
  Copy and complete the chart.

Place name	Where it comes from

- Research present place names by looking in local history books.

SPECIALS! Study Skills

Structure - the shape of poetry

● Describe these buildings. How are they made? What is their shape?

● With your Study Buddy describe the 'shape' of the three poems below.
● Do the poems have a reason for their shape?
● Write words that describe their shape, in the spaces around them.

The river
   ran by
      the banks
       so high
     travelling fast
     travelling
       free
        taking me
   home

Ben was wise
He was no fool
(Yet he had never spent a day at school)
Jim was good
At school all day
(He still can't spell unto this day).

Despise
Conceit
Liar
Cheat
Right to the end
He had no friend

● With your Study Buddy, choose two poems.
● Describe their shape to each other.
● Why do you think the poet chose his or her structure?

       SPECIALS! Study Skills   © Folens

People and style

- With your Study Buddy, think of words to describe the style of the four people below.

- How might they talk? Write their words in the speech bubbles.

1. VERILY I SAY UNTO YOU. COME FORTH UNTO THE GARDEN. LO AND BEHOLD. AMEN.

2.

3.

4.

- Write about three of the people. Use the speech bubbles to help you.
- Talk about what 'style' means.

SPECIALS! Study Skills

Style in writing

- Read this newspaper report:

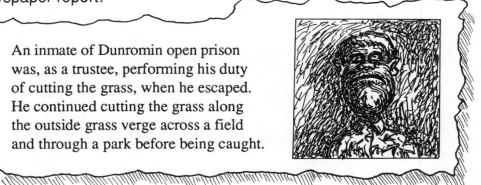

An inmate of Dunromin open prison was, as a trustee, performing his duty of cutting the grass, when he escaped. He continued cutting the grass along the outside grass verge across a field and through a park before being caught.

- How might a police sergeant have reported this? Write your version below.

MY STUDY BUDDY IS

- Ask your Study Buddy to write below how a seven-year-old might have written it.

NoW

- Compare your reports.
- What is different about the ways they are written? Why?
- Can you tell your Study Buddy what 'style' is in writing?

- Choose a short newspaper report with your Study Buddy. Re-write it in another style.

SPECIALS! Study Skills   © Folens

Putting it together

This poem has been jumbled up.

- Cut out the lines. With your Study Buddy put the lines back together until they make sense.
  - Do you need to divide it into verses?
  - What structure or 'shape' seems best?
  - Read the poem aloud.
  - How would you describe the style it is written in? Why?

Shall be trod by beasts alone

Beast of England, beast of Ireland

Soon or late the day is coming

Of the golden future time

Beasts of every land and clime

And the fruitful fields of England

Harken to my joyful tidings

Tyrant man shall be o'er thrown

- Choose a poem and copy each line on to a separate card.
  Ask your Study Buddy to put it together.
- Compare it with the original. Is it the same? If not, does it matter?

Persuasive language

- Sell your Study Buddy the latest anti-spot face cream 'Banzit'.
- Try flattery to start with! Here is some 'flatter patter':

"If you care about yourself ...."
"If you deserve the best ...."
"Are you someone special? Then ...."

- Write some more flatter patter starters below.

- Here are some 'emotional starters'. Add your own in the box below.

"No friends? Still ...."
"Left out of the party again? ...."
"Home alone at your age? ...."

- Look at some magazine advertisements with your Study Buddy.
- How do they try to appeal to you? List five different ways.

SPECIALS! Study Skills © Folens

Headlines

● Read this part of a newspaper article:

... the man threatened to attack the local police officer as he resisted arrest. He refused to get into the car and shouted abuse at passers by ...

● Make up a headline for the extract. Write it below.

● Write a beginning and an end to the extract.
  Use the space below. Think about:
  – who is the man?
  – how old is he?
● Ask your Study Buddy to do the same.
● Is your headline still suitable?

● Collect two headlines from newspapers. Do not read the articles.
● With your Studdy Buddy, write an article that would suit each headline.
● Read the articles and compare yours with the real thing!

SPECIALS! Study Skills

Angles

How do people persuade you to buy something? They use an 'angle'.

● Underline the words in this advertisement that would influence you to buy a car.

This must be the best buy of the century. Economical on fuel, it will save you pounds. Think of all the other things you can do with the cash. Don't waste your hard-earned money by even considering any other car. This one leaves a smile on your face – and a smile on you bank manager's, too.

● What angle are they using to sell this car?

● Choose one of the angles below.
● Let your Study Buddy choose one as well.
● Write a new advertisement to persuade people to buy a car.
● Compare your advertisements.

LOOKS
FASHION
LEISURE
YOUTH

SPEED
freedom
TRAVEL
COLOUR

● Look at some car magazines with your Study Buddy.
  Select three car advertisements. List their angles for selling.
● Which angle is most used in car selling?

SPECIALS! Study Skills   © Folens

Giving your opinion

● Read this extract:

Traffic jams are a constant source of concern in the area. Delays are frequent and the possibility of road widening cannot be considered. "The only solution is to encourage more people to ride motorbikes," said a local resident. "They are fast, efficient and take up less room."

● Discuss which resident might have made the comment above.
● Describe that person below. Compare your opinions.

● Decide who might have made these comments:

"We need a skateboarding area."

"We want more late night cafe's."

"There are not enough nursery schools."

● Who would *not* have made them?

● Look at the picture. Discuss with your Study Buddy who might want a new church built on Praymor Village Green and who would definitely not.

SPECIALS! Study Skills

Skimming and scanning

Look at the advertisement. Read this question:
How long will I wait for a bay window, once ordered?

STEP ONE: *Skim* through this information for an idea of what it contains.

STEP TWO: Look at the title and key points that would answer the question (that is, *scan* it).

WINDOW SALE OF THE SEASON

Our Trumpton Factory is
open to the public
8.30am – 5pm Mon to Sat.
No-obligation discussions.
Patio doors, bay windows,
conservatories and porches.
Delivery in 4–6 weeks.
Also available in Georgian
and lead design.
Why wait 6–8 weeks for
superstores to deliver?

- Now write your answer to the
  question at the top of this page here:

- Write below how you looked for the answer.

- Find a page from a school book with questions at the end. Take one question, highlight its important parts.
- Read the page to find the answer.
- Tell your Study Buddy why it helped to read the question first.

Search-reading

- Match a company to each advertisement. Give reasons for your choice.

... superb, mouthwatering dishes, air-conditioned restaurant ...

All types and sizes of wood supplied.

Shaping – Pruning – Trimming FREE ESTIMATES

Massage, aromatherapy sportswear, yoga – something for everyone.

Every size in stock of
Dunlop
Goodyear
Pirelli and
Michelin

Wake up to the common-sense approach to exercise and nutrition

- Ask your Study Buddy to search for something in a newspaper.
  For instance:
  - the television page
  - your horoscope.
- Talk about whether they were easy to find and why.

Intensive reading

● Read this information:

> Welcome to Mendit Hospital. You are in the main entrance. To reach the X-ray department, go out of the doors by the sweet counter, turn right and continue until you reach the lift. Take the lift to the second floor. Go left out of the lift and down the corridor past the turning for Todd ward. The x-ray department is on the right.

● How *do* you reach the X-ray department? Draw your route below:

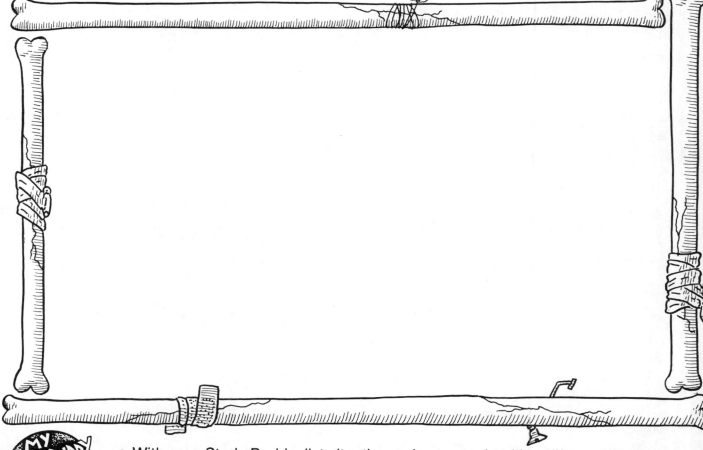

● With your Study Buddy, list situations where your health or life could be in danger if you do not read instructions intensively. Say why this could be.
● What kinds of things would you need to highlight in 'life or death' instructions? List these with your Study Buddy.

SPECIALS! Study Skills

Using clues

Look at this picture and story title. They provide clues about the story.

- List below what you think the story is about.
- Ask your Study Buddy to do the same. Do you both agree?

[box]

- Clues can be obtained from other words. Write in the missing words here:

A ghostly flame flickered from the tall ....

It was the .... blackest bird I'd ever seen.

I was soaked by the pounding ....

His eyes were like .... drawing me to him.

- Discuss what words would definitely *not* be expected!

- Choose a book with your Study Buddy. List unfamiliar words from the first three pages.
- Can you work out their meanings from the other words around them? Explain to your Study Buddy how you do this.

Revision of a topic

- Choose a topic for revision.
- Let your Study Buddy test you by asking the 'Wh' words!

TOPIC:

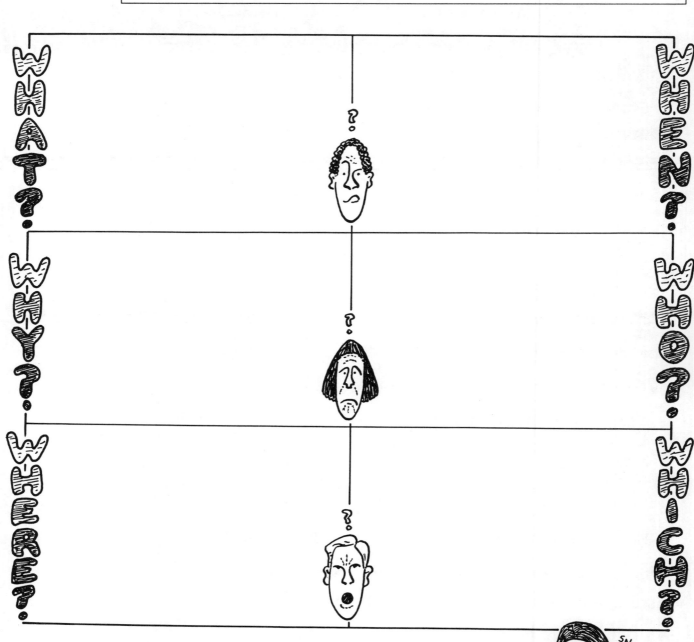

WHAT?

WHY?

WHERE?

WHEN?

WHO?

WHICH?

- Swap over. Who remembered most?
- Can you work out why?
- How useful was your Study Skills Kit?

Memory triggers - labelling

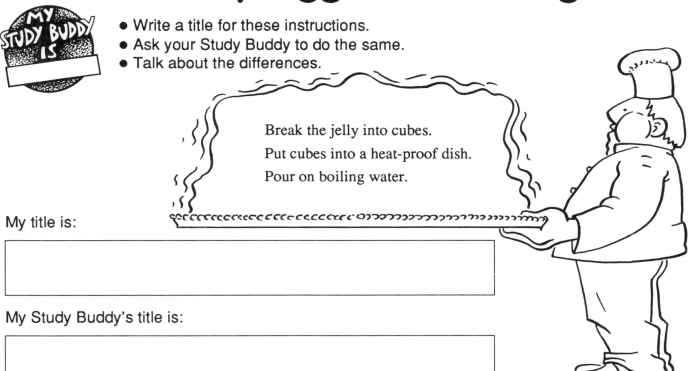

- Write a title for these instructions.
- Ask your Study Buddy to do the same.
- Talk about the differences.

MY STUDY BUDDY IS

Break the jelly into cubes.
Put cubes into a heat-proof dish.
Pour on boiling water.

My title is:

My Study Buddy's title is:

- Label this extract:

The school expects certain standards of behaviour from pupils. If the school rules are broken, pupils will, on the first occasion be given a warning slip.

My title is:

My Study Buddy's title is:

- Choose a book that you and your Study Buddy need to revise from.
- Select one chapter. Use your Post-its to make a title or label for each page.
- Detach your Post-its. Let your Study Buddy read them to you.
- How much of each page can you remember?

Memory triggers - setting questions

- Read this piece of writing with your Study Buddy.

A renewed crisis in the coal industry might have been foreseen and should have been forestalled. The foreign demand for British coal fell off sharply, especially with the recovery of the Ruhr, so that prices, profits and wages declined. The mine owners asked for still further reductions in wages to enable them to meet foreign competition, but the miners were determined to have "not a minute on the day, not a penny off the pay".

- Make up one question each about the passage.
- Write them below.

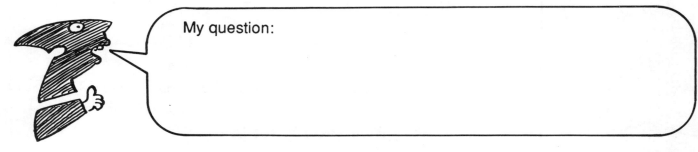

My question:

My Study Buddy's question:

- Talk about what you needed to do in order to find a question.
- Did you notice how you had to read and re-read the passage to make up a really good question?

- With your Study Buddy, choose a piece of work you need to revise.
- Using cards from the Study Skills Kit, make a pack of seven questions.
- Ask the questions to see how much information you can remember.

SPECIALS! Study Skills © Folens

Memory triggers - giving answers

- Choose a piece of information that you need to revise.
- Ask your Study Buddy to write questions, one for each card below.
- Read the answers then draw the answers.

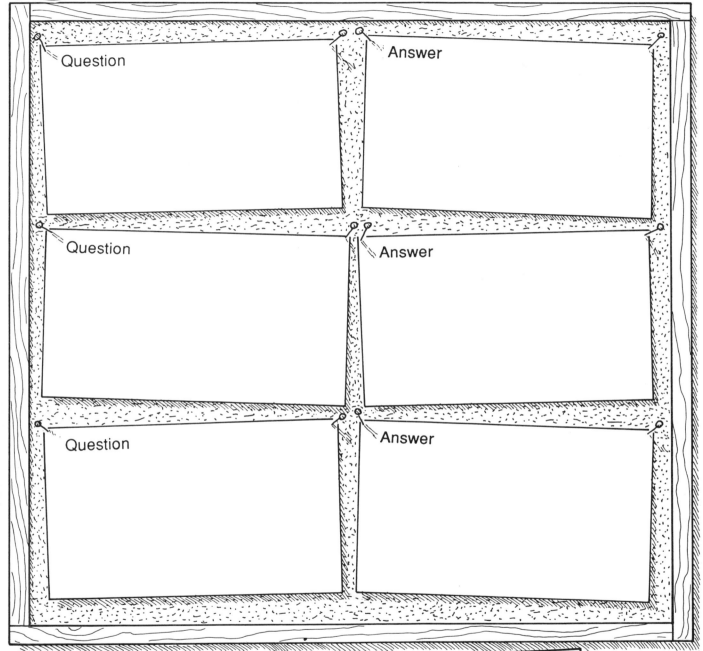

Question

Answer

Question

Answer

Question

Answer

- Use this method to make sets of revision packs for two subjects.
  Use the cards from your Study Skills Kit.
- Think of seven questions before you read to find your answers!

My History Revision Pack

- Make a title card for each of your revision packs so that you can find the pack you need at any time.

SPECIALS! Study Skills

Memory triggers - mnemonics

- Read this sentence:

  Before **p**lanting **s**wedes **c**offee **m**akes **a** **b**reak.

- Why could it help you to remember to buy:

  Beetroot **p**arsnip **s**wede **c**abbage **m**arrow **a**pples **b**roccoli?

- With your Study Buddy, think up a way to remember the following words:

  evaporation, perspiration, transpiration, respiration,

- Write your sentence (or rhyme) on small cards. These are called 'nudge cards'. Why do you think they are called this?
- Test each other.

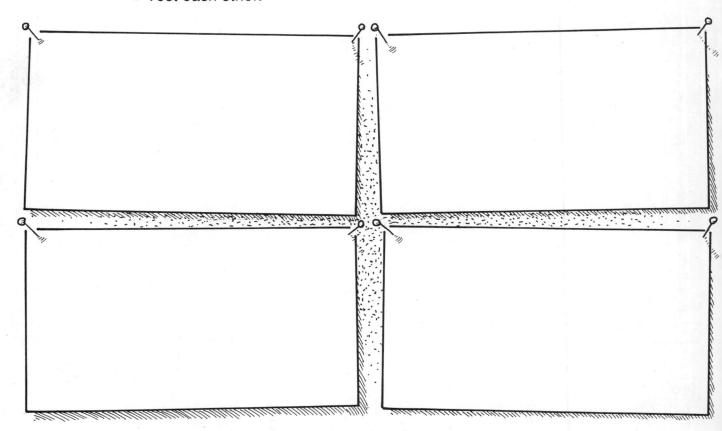

- With your Study Buddy, choose something you need to remember, such as:
  - characters in a play
  - chemicals in an experiment.
- Make a set of nudge cards and test each other.

SPECIALS! Study Skills